CREMATION

WHAT GOD TELL US?

By

Juan F. Negron

AuthorHouse™
1663 Liberty Drive
Bloomington, IN 47403
www.authorhouse.com
Phone: 833-262-8899

All scripture is taken from King James Version of the Bible.

Scripture quotations marked KJV are from the Holy Bible, King James Version (Authorized Version). First published in 1611. Quoted from the KJV Classic Reference Bible, Copyright © 1983 by The Zondervan Corporation.

This book is printed on acid-free paper.

ISBN: 979-8-8230-2927-8 (sc)
ISBN: 979-8-8230-2928-5 (e)

Library of Congress Control Number: 2024913287

Print information available on the last page.

Published by AuthorHouse 12/16/2024

authorHOUSE

Contents

Preface

My mind is based more on science. After graduating from high school, I embarked on a journey in chemical engineering technology. I then earned my bachelor's degree in chemistry and also became a science teacher for middle and high school students. When I was in elementary school, I stopped believing in the Bible. As I mentioned above, my mind was more oriented toward science. During my day to day life/struggles/experiences with not only my family as a child/adult, my collegues but also my self as an individual. I had questions and looking for answers in my daily life in every situation since I was a child.

Thinking back, it was right after high school that I decided to give God an opportunity to show me that the scriptures shown on the Bible are real and not a legend. Once I opened my heart to the possibility, things started to happen in my life that I could not explain. Because God is Gracious and has manifested His Glory in me countless times, I have more than one testimony that I could share with you. For the purpose of this book, I will mention only one of them for it would take pages and pages to share my spiritual experiences and the main focus here is cremation.

A few years back, my wife and I were very active in a church. I was in the music ministry as I have played piano since I was in the fifth grade. My wife and I prepare the room for the service at the church. We made sure that everthing was in order and ready to welcome everyone. Once in a while I had the opportunity to preach in English and Spanish for different churches. The church that we use to go is about one hour from our home. It was during a winter that a miracle happened. This miracle was very impressive that marked my wife and I forever. Let me explain. My wife and I have a tendency to wake up around 4:00 am. On this particular day, my wife came to our room and told me that I needed to get out of the bed and see what was happening in our home. In a moment of panic, I thought something terrible was happening. As I made my way out of the room and kept walking towards the hallway, I noticed a light on the ceiling, walls, and floor of our living room. This light had the colors of the rainbow, but in a perfect small circle, the size of a golf ball. It was 4:00 am and the house was dark, there was no way to explain what I was seeing expect His way of showing us that He was with us in that very moment. We have been in our home over third years, we have never seen anything like this. Picture a disco ball when the light hits the ball you will see hundreds of tiny lights around the room. Well, that was exactly what we had in our room, but instead of a light it was hundreds of tiny rainbows. My wife and I bend knee when we saw it. We have all seen or felt the beauty of Him. I believe if you are reading this book you have seen or felt Him also.

Getting back on the topic, I took classes to become a pastor. However, God was preparing me for a journey full of challenges and blessings.

Believing in God is not enough. Walking in the doctrine of God is what makes the difference. What I am and who I am- My wonderful wife, who is a believer and full in Christ our Lord, my children, my faith —is part of my blessings and rewards. I give thanks to Christ our Lord. We have three children and ten grandchildren. It's wonderful! What a blessing it is.

My walk was based on a determination to see the work and feel the presence of God the Creator, His Son, and the Holy Spirit. I had to be honest with myself and dare to surrender my life into the hands of God. For many decades, I thought cremation was OK, but God knew when and how to get me to see His point of view.

This topic teaches us to live in God and with God when we walk by faith. During the reading, you will find scriptures that come from the Bible. I have not altered the sacred writing. You will see it in red <u>words</u>.

Introduction

As a Christian, I thought that cremation was accepted. A few years ago, I began to have doubts. One day, The Holy Trinity—The Father, who is the Creator of everything, The Verb (Son) and The Holy Spirit—managed to provide me with a small pamphlet in which cremation was discussed. When I finished reading it, I was surprised. I was looking at it from **my** point of view, but it did not occur to me to see it from GODS point of view. Something in my heart was telling me that I had to pass this information on to other believers.

Don't let other people, cultures, traditions, or financial problems tempt you into a psychological trap. Your decision must be based on your discernment. It's not based on what your parents and siblings decided or because your husband or wife wants it that way. Also, you should not get carried away by excuses to justify yourself and then say, "I did this because they advised me to," or "I did this because most people do it."

In order to understand the concept of cremation, to understand what God is telling us, and to learn at what moments God uses fire to burn and destroy, we must take into account some basic concepts as believers.

There is a divine reason why all things were written into the sacred scriptures. What was written is for our learning.

For whatsoever things were written aforetime were written for our learning, that we through patience and comfort of the scriptures might have hope. (Romans 15:4 KJV)

In *Webster's Ninth New Collegiate Dictionary*, the word *cremation* means "to burn up, cremate; to reduce (as a dead body) to ashes by burning." From the book of "Cremation – Is it Christian?" mention that the *Britannica Encyclopedia* indicating that the cremation is the burning of human corpus which was the general practice of the ancient world, with the important exceptions of Egypt, where bodies were embalmed; Judea (or Ancient Israel) where they were buried in sepulchers, and China, where they were buried in the earth.

According to the *Encyclopedia Britannica*, cremation is still practiced greatly in parts of Asia and America, but it's not always in the same form. Ashes may be stored in urns, buried in the earth, thrown to the wind, or as among the Digger Indians, smeared with gum on the heads of the mourners.

Modern crematories are specially constructed buildings erected for the purpose of the incineration of human bodies. They have individual compartments that are heated to a temperature that quickly reduces the body to ashes. When the heat (two thousand degrees Fahrenheit) becomes intense, the body appears to be very much alive as it jumps about, which is the result of the contraction and expansion of the muscles. The remaining ashes' weight is around three to four pounds. Something that can be said in favor of cremation is that it may be less expensive than a burial because a cemetery lot is unnecessary; although some do bury the ashes.

There are two basic reasons that some believers practice the cremation.

1. Historically, cremation has been associated with the efforts of unbelievers in their denial of the resurrection of the body.

2. The cremation is for aesthetic, sanitary, or economic reasons.

It is not difficult to understand why people who are not well acquainted with the holy scriptures lend their support to this pagan practice. If people were more knowledgeable on the Bible, I am sure that they would be more careful with the remains of their loved ones and even their own. According to divine standards, it was a supreme dishonor and curse for a person to have no burial. No person of any academic standing can find one sentence of scripture to support the burning of the bodies of honorable Christian people.

Reflection

And ye shall know the truth, and the truth shall make you free. (John 8:32)

There they cry, but none giveth answer, because of the pride of evil men. (Job 35:12)

Note

The words in quotes are obtained from the Bible. They have not been corrected or altered. At the end of this book, you can find the scriptures that have been mentioned. There are believers who think that the Old Testament is obsolete and that it has expired. However, the New Testament tells us that the covenant that God made with the Jewish people expired, not because God is imperfect but because human beings violated the contract. In other words, the law follows every teaching that helps us become good believers and servants of God, and it is not obsolete. We see this in the Bible.

6But now hath he obtained a more excellent ministry, by how much also he is the mediator of a better covenant, which was established upon better promises. 7For if that first covenant had been faultless, then should no place have been sought for the second. 8For finding fault with them, he saith, Behold, the days come, saith the Lord, when I will make a new covenant with the house of Israel and with the house of Judah: 9Not according to the covenant that I made with their fathers in the day when I took them by the hand to lead them out of the land of Egypt; because they continued not in my covenant, and I regarded them not, saith the Lord. 10For this is the covenant that I will make with the house of Israel after those days, saith the Lord; I will put my laws into their mind, and write them in their hearts: and I will be to them a God, and they shall be to me a people: 11And they shall not teach every man his neighbour, and every man his brother, saying, Know the Lord: for all shall know me, from the least to the greatest. 12For I will be merciful to their unrighteousness, and their sins and their iniquities will I remember no more. 13In that he saith, A new covenant, he hath made the first old. Now that which decayeth and waxeth old is ready to vanish away. (Hebrews 8:6–13)

[17]Think not that I am come to destroy the law, or the prophets: I am not come to destroy, but to fulfil. 18For verily I say unto you, Till heaven and earth pass, one jot or one tittle shall in no wise pass from the law, till all be fulfilled. 19Whosoever therefore shall break one of these least commandments, and shall teach men so, he shall be called the least in the kingdom of heaven: but whosoever shall do and teach them, the same shall be called great in the kingdom of heaven. [20]For I say unto you, That except your righteousness shall exceed the righteousness of the scribes and Pharisees, ye shall in no case enter into the kingdom of heaven. (Matthew 5:17–20)

[25]But this cometh to pass, that the word might be fulfilled that is written in their law, They hated me without a cause. [26]But when the Comforter is come, whom I will send unto you from the Father, even the Spirit of truth, which proceedeth from the Father, he shall testify of me: [27]And ye also shall bear witness, because ye have been with me from the beginning. (John 15:25–27)

Do You Not Know that Your Body Is the Temple of the Holy Spirit, Who Is in You and Whom You Have From God, And that You Are Not Your Own?

¹⁹What? know ye not that your body is the temple of the Holy Ghost which is in you, which ye have of God, and ye are not your own? ²⁰For ye are bought with a price: therefore glorify God in your body, and in your spirit, which are God's. (1 Corinthians 6:19–20)

This text plainly states that our bodies are not our own to do with as we please.

In Genesis 3:19, God said, "In the sweat of thy face shalt thou eat bread, till thou return unto the ground; for out of it wast thou taken: for dust thou art, and unto dust shalt thou return." According to divine precept and example, there is but one Christian way to dispose of our dead, and that is to bury them.

¹Ye are the children of the LORD your God: ye shall not cut yourselves, nor make any baldness between your eyes for the dead. 2For thou art an holy people unto the LORD thy God, and the LORD hath chosen thee to be a peculiar people unto himself, above all the nations that are upon the earth. (Deuteronomy 14:1–2)

And the very God of peace sanctify you wholly; and I pray God your whole spirit and soul and body be preserved blameless unto the coming of our Lord Jesus Christ. (1 Thessalonians 5:23)

If you want God to sanctify your body, remember that by intentionally burning your body, the body is destroyed. You have not preserved the body so that one day God can raise, resurrect, and change the body (see 1 Corinthians 15:51-52). This scripture specifically elaborates on the rapture of the church. Dead bodies will be raised, and as the body go to the sky, the body will change to be raised incorruptible. For the corruptible body shall be put on incorruptible, and the mortal body shall have put on immortality.

Numbers of People in the Bible Were Cursed for Their Disobedience to God

And it shall be, that he that is taken with the accursed thing shall be burnt with fire, he and all that he hath: because he hath transgressed the covenant of the LORD, and because he hath wrought folly in Israel. (Joshua 7:15)

Thus saith the LORD; For three transgressions of Moab, and for four, I will not turn away the punishment thereof; because he burned the bones of the king of Edom into lime. (Amos 2:1)

[16]And as Josiah turned himself, he spied the sepulchres that were there in the mount, and sent, and took the bones out of the sepulchres, and burned them upon the altar, and polluted it, according to the word of the LORD which the man of God proclaimed, who proclaimed these words. [17]Then he said, What title is that that I see? And the men of the city told him, It is the sepulchre of the man of God, which came from Judah, and proclaimed these things that thou hast done against the altar of Bethel. [18]And he said, Let him alone; let no man move his bones. So they let his bones alone, with the bones of the prophet that came out of Samaria. [19]And all the houses also of the high places that were in the cities of Samaria, which the kings of Israel had made to provoke the LORD to anger, Josiah took away, and did to them according to all the acts that he had done in Bethel. [20]And he slew all the priests of the high places that were there upon the altars, and burned men's bones upon them, and returned to Jerusalem. (2 Kings 23:16–20)

Cremation Is of Heathen Origin

Let's look at an example from India. Cremation is a common practice among the Hindus, but the Muslims bury their dead.

James W. Fraser (minister of the gospel since 1921) asked a missionary from India if the Christians of that land cremated their dead. With a look of surprise, he said, "Positively not! Cremation is heathen. The Christians of India bury their dead, because burial is Christian." There is absolutely nothing Christian about cremation. It is as pagan as idol worship.

Cremation Is an Aid to Crime

By those who are in a position to know, it has been stated by the police department, that a proper analysis cannot be obtained after the cremation of a human body. As a scientist I can agree with this. The reason is because at high temperature the chemical structure is transform to another chemical structure which cannot be related to the original chemical structure. Therefore, it is a positive aid to crime.

Cremation is Anti-Biblical and Unchristian

You are not your own. (1 Corinthians 6:19–20)

The sense of divine ownership rather than self-ownership is the inspiration of all Christian dignity and strength. The doctrine of the resurrection reminds us that the body is not to be treated as a temporary thing or as belonging to this stage of existence only.

Rather than give our consent to destroy God's property in the oven of a crematorium, every loved one should be affectionately and carefully laid away whole in Mother Earth like the body of our Savior. His body was lovingly and tenderly prepared for burial according to the customs of God's people (see John 19:38–42). The Hebrew people considered all burial grounds sacred and marked the place where each body was interred.

Perhaps one of the reasons why some Christians have had their loved ones' bodies cremated is that many preachers have failed to teach the great Bible doctrine regarding the sanctity of a Christian's body. This is a very grave omission, for in Malachi 2:7, we read, "For the priest's lips should keep knowledge, and they should seek the law at his mouth: for he is the messenger of the LORD of hosts."

The teaching of the sacredness regarding the bodies of God's people is carried into the New Testament. It is enjoined upon Christians everywhere in such portions as 1 Corinthians 6:15–20 and Romans 6:13; 12:1. (See the content of these scriptures at the end of this book or look for them in your own Bible.) In Romans 14:8, the apostle Paul says, "For whether we live, we live unto the Lord; and whether we die, we die unto the Lord: whether we live therefore, or die, we are the Lord's." Christianity not only concerns itself with the soul but also with the body, for both will be redeemed.

And not only they, but ourselves also, which have the first fruits of the Spirit, even we ourselves groan within ourselves, waiting for the adoption, to wit, the redemption of our body. (Romans 8:23)

In 1886, the Roman Catholic Church officially banned this gruesome practice. Long before that date, however, Baptist pastors and their congregations spoke against and abhorred this pagan rite. It's not only these people. Any group of people who accepts the Bible as the Word of God and as its criterion for faith and practice can only condemn this heathen way of disposing of a Christian's body.

However, in 1963, Pope Paul VI officially approved the practice of cremation. Other Christian churches accept it as well. Every Christian church that supports cremation has its own rules regarding cremation.

I can speculate that these churches accept cremation because they are afraid of losing members, which means losing money and power over believers. The same thing happened when in the Old Testament, the believers started to mix with pagans and even had idols. Today is no different. Some churches provide new doctrines because we are living in a different time and a modern world. God's words from the past, present, and future will always be the same. The world changes (technology and the way people are living), but people are the same. One of the differences between those living in the past and present is their knowledge.

Cremation Is Contrary to the Example and Teachings of Jesus and the Christian Church

There are believers saying, "There is nothing in The Holy Scriptures that forbids cremation." Let's start by saying that Jesus Christ came to this world to fulfill the scriptures. During His walk on Earth, He showed us the way that Christians should address their lives—in the same way that He did it.

That Jesus Himself was buried was not a coincidence or an accident. Jesus Christ was buried because burial was in harmony with God's purposes.

And he made his grave with the wicked, and with the rich in his death; because he had done no violence, neither was any deceit in his mouth. (Isaiah 53:9)

By the which will we are sanctified through the offering of the body of Jesus Christ once for all. (Hebrews 10:10)

[57]When the even was come, there came a rich man of Arimathaea, named Joseph, who also himself was Jesus' disciple: [58]He went to Pilate, and begged the body of Jesus. Then Pilate commanded the body to be delivered. [59]And when Joseph had taken the body, he wrapped it in a clean linen cloth, [60]And laid it in his own new tomb, which he had hewn out in the rock: and he rolled a great stone to the door of the sepulchre, and departed. (Mathew 27:57–60)

What Happens to the Soul of a Believer when He or She Is Cremated?

The first thing we have to keep in mind is that no one can judge anyone else. No one can say that someone is going to hell or paradise. God warns us about judging. The only thing we can say is what Jesus told us. For example, Jesus told us that anyone who believed in Jesus would have eternal life. In other words, a person identifies Jesus as his or her Savior. So, we can say that at the moment of a believer's death, he or she will immediately goes to paradise, regardless of whether the body is cremated or not.

The problem begins for the one who cremates the body. We see that God does not like a body to be burned regardless of whether the person is a believer or not. We see that God punishes the person who cremates the body. See Joshua 7:15 & Amos 2:1)

The person who cremated the body has options. The person may or may not regret having cremated a body. Jesus will look into that person's heart and judge if the person has repented or not. One thing is clear: No one can say to God, "I did not know," because ignorance does not exempt him or her from guilt. In fact, God alerts us that through ignorance, God's people will perish.

My people are destroyed for lack of knowledge: because thou hast rejected knowledge, I will also reject thee, that thou shalt be no priest to me: seeing thou hast forgotten the law of thy God, I will also forget thy children. (Hosea 4:6)

There they cry, but none giveth answer, because of the pride of evil men. (Job 35:12)

The important thing is that the believer does the things that please the Lord. If for some reason, that individual doesn't have the budget to pay for the burial, that person should ask God to guide and help him or her to make a wise decision. For example, the first thing a person looks for is an expensive coffin. It does not have to be this way. Find a simple coffin. There are multiple types of services, which may incur a lower or higher cost. You can find a service that fits your families needs/budget. Anyway, there are many ways to find a solution to the problem.

Conclusion

We observe that the holy scriptures teach us the following:

1. Our bodies are the temples of the Holy Spirit (1 Corinthians 6:19).

2. Our bodies are the members of Christ (1 Corinthians 6:15).

3. Self-ownership is a pagan concept. If we want to live in the will of God, we are not free to do with our bodies as we please (1 Corinthians 6:20).

4. Dead or alive, our bodies belong to God because of redemption and sanctification (Romans 8:23 and Hebrews 10:10).

5. The Christian way of disposing of our dead is by burial only, as exemplified in sacred history.

6. Our bodies are the seed of our resurrection bodies (1 Corinthians 15:38).

7. God does not approve of the burning of human bodies—not even of our enemies. This was one of Moab's unpardoned sins (Amos 2:1).

8. Cremation has come to us from the uncivilized, uncultured, pagan people of the Dark Ages. This custom is positively unrefined, unholy, and pagan.

9. Cremation is of heathen origin, an aid to crime, a barbarous act, anti-biblical, and therefore, unchristian.

10. God shall burn the carved images of their gods with fire. Deuteronomy 7:25 showed that in God's sight, cremation was the most dishonorable of all disposals. It says, "The graven images of their gods shall ye burn with fire: thou shalt not desire the silver or gold that is on them, nor take it unto thee, lest thou be snared therein: for it is an abomination to the LORD thy God."

11. Again, the following verse shows that cremation was, in God's sight, the most dishonorable of all disposals: And it shall be, that he that is taken with the accursed thing shall be burnt with fire, he and all that he hath: because he hath transgressed the covenant of the LORD, and because he hath wrought folly in Israel. (Joshua 7:15).

12. These two scriptures (Deuteronomy 7:25 and Joshua 7:15) were the laws of God. We see how it was obeyed by David and his men in 1 Chronicles 14:12 and by Jehu in 2 Kings 10:26. Also, during the life of Moses, an incident was recorded in Exodus 32:1–24 as to how this was done.

13. There is a divine reason why the account in Romans 15:4 was written into the sacred scriptures. The things that were written long ago are for our learning.

Summary

1. Cremation is contrary to the example and teachings of Jesus and the church.

2. Cremation supremely dishonors a redeemed body.

3. Cremation destroys the sacred memory of our beloved dead.

4. Cremation is contrary to the biblical and historical record.

For Meditation and Guidance

If any of you lack wisdom, let him ask of God, that giveth to all men liberally, and upbraideth not; and it shall be given him. (James 1:5)

Bible Scriptures from the Old Testament

In the sweat of thy face shalt thou eat bread, till thou return unto the ground; for out of it wast thou taken: for dust thou art, and unto dust shalt thou return. **(Genesis 3:19)**

[1]And when the people saw that Moses delayed to come down out of the mount, the people gathered themselves together unto Aaron, and said unto him, Up, make us gods, which shall go before us; for as for this Moses, the man that brought us up out of the land of Egypt, we wot not what is become of him. [2]And Aaron said unto them, Break off the golden earrings, which are in the ears of your wives, of your sons, and of your daughters, and bring them unto me. [3]And all the people brake off the golden earrings which were in their ears, and brought them unto Aaron. [4]And he received them at their hand, and fashioned it with a graving tool, after he had made it a molten calf: and they said, These be thy gods, O Israel, which brought thee up out of the land of Egypt. [5]And when Aaron saw it, he built an altar before it; and Aaron made proclamation, and said, To morrow is a feast to the LORD. [6]And they rose up early on the morrow, and offered burnt offerings, and brought peace offerings; and the people sat down to eat and to drink, and rose up to play. [7]And the LORD said unto Moses, Go, get thee down; for thy people, which thou broughtest out of the land of Egypt, have corrupted themselves: [8]They have turned aside quickly out of the way which I commanded them: they have made them a molten calf, and have worshipped it, and have sacrificed thereunto, and said, These be thy gods, O Israel, which have brought thee up out of the land of Egypt. [9]And the LORD said unto Moses, I have seen this people, and, behold, it is a stiffnecked people: [10]Now therefore let me alone, that my wrath may wax hot against them, and that I may consume them: and I will make of thee a great nation. [11]And Moses besought the LORD his God, and said, LORD, why doth thy wrath wax hot against thy people, which thou hast brought forth out of the land of Egypt with great power, and with a mighty hand? [12]Wherefore should the Egyptians speak, and say, For mischief did he bring them out, to slay them in the mountains, and to consume them from the face of the earth? Turn from thy fierce wrath, and repent of this evil against thy people. [13]Remember Abraham, Isaac, and Israel,

thy servants, to whom thou swarest by thine own self, and saidst unto them, I will multiply your seed as the stars of heaven, and all this land that I have spoken of will I give unto your seed, and they shall inherit it for ever. ¹⁴ And the LORD repented of the evil which he thought to do unto his people.

¹⁵And Moses turned, and went down from the mount, and the two tables of the testimony were in his hand: the tables were written on both their sides; on the one side and on the other were they written. ¹⁶And the tables were the work of God, and the writing was the writing of God, graven upon the tables. ¹⁷And when Joshua heard the noise of the people as they shouted, he said unto Moses, There is a noise of war in the camp. ¹⁸And he said, It is not the voice of them that shout for mastery, neither is it the voice of them that cry for being overcome: but the noise of them that sing do I hear. ¹⁹And it came to pass, as soon as he came nigh unto the camp, that he saw the calf, and the dancing: and Moses' anger waxed hot, and he cast the tables out of his hands, and brake them beneath the mount. ²⁰And he took the calf which they had made, and burnt it in the fire, and ground it to powder, and strawed it upon the water, and made the children of Israel drink of it. ²¹And Moses said unto Aaron, What did this people unto thee, that thou hast brought so great a sin upon them? ²²And Aaron said, Let not the anger of my lord wax hot: thou knowest the people, that they are set on mischief. ²³For they said unto me, Make us gods, which shall go before us: for as for this Moses, the man that brought us up out of the land of Egypt, we wot not what is become of him. ²⁴And I said unto them, Whosoever hath any gold, let them break it off. So they gave it me: then I cast it into the fire, and there came out this calf. (Exodus 32:1–24)

The graven images of their gods shall ye burn with fire: thou shalt not desire the silver or gold that is on them, nor take it unto thee, lest thou be snared therein: for it is an abomination to the LORD thy God. (Deuteronomy 7:25)

1Ye are the children of the LORD your God: ye shall not cut yourselves, nor make any baldness between your eyes for the dead. 2For thou art an holy people unto the LORD thy God, and the LORD hath chosen thee to be a peculiar people unto himself, above all the nations that are upon the earth. (Deuteronomy 14:1–2)

And it shall be, that he that is taken with the accursed thing shall be burnt with fire, he and all that he hath: because he hath transgressed the covenant of the LORD, and because he hath wrought folly in Israel. (Joshua 7:15)

And they brought forth the images out of the house of Baal, and burned them. (2 Kings 10:26)

¹⁶And as Josiah turned himself, he spied the sepulchres that were there in the mount, and sent, and took the bones out of the sepulchres, and burned them upon the altar, and polluted it, according to the word of the LORD which the man of God proclaimed, who proclaimed these words. ¹⁷Then he said, What title is that that I see? And the men of the city told him, It is the sepulchre of the man of God, which came from Judah, and proclaimed these things that thou hast done against the altar of Bethel. ¹⁸And he said, Let him alone; let no man move his bones. So they let his bones alone, with the bones of the prophet that came out of Samaria. ¹⁹And all the houses also of the high places that were in the cities of Samaria, which the kings of Israel had made to provoke the LORD to anger, Josiah took away, and did to them according to all the acts that he had done in Bethel. ²⁰And he slew all the priests of the high places that were there upon the altars, and burned men's bones upon them, and returned to Jerusalem. (2 Kings 23:16–20)

And when they had left their gods there, David gave a commandment, and they were burned with fire. (1 Chronicles 14:12)

There they cry, but none giveth answer, because of the pride of evil men. (Job 35:12)

And he made his grave with the wicked, and with the rich in his death; because he had done no violence, neither was any deceit in his mouth. (Isaiah 53:9)

My people are destroyed for lack of knowledge: because thou hast rejected knowledge, I will also reject thee, that thou shalt be no priest to me: seeing thou hast forgotten the law of thy God, I will also forget thy children. (Hosea 4:6)

Thus saith the LORD; For three transgressions of Moab, and for four, I will not turn away the punishment thereof; because he burned the bones of the king of Edom into lime. (Amos 2:1)

For the priest's lips should keep knowledge, and they should seek the law at his mouth: for he is the messenger of the LORD of hosts. (Malachi 2:7)

Bible Scriptures from the New Testament

[17]Think not that I am come to destroy the law, or the prophets: I am not come to destroy, but to fulfil. [18]For verily I say unto you, Till heaven and earth pass, one jot or one tittle shall in no wise pass from the law, till all be fulfilled. [19]Whosoever therefore shall break one of these least commandments, and shall teach men so, he shall be called the least in the kingdom of heaven: but whosoever shall do and teach them, the same shall be called great in the kingdom of heaven. [20]For I say unto you, That except your righteousness shall exceed the righteousness of the scribes and Pharisees, ye shall in no case enter into the kingdom of heaven. (Matthew 5:17–20)

[57]When the even was come, there came a rich man of Arimathaea, named Joseph, who also himself was Jesus' disciple: [58]He went to Pilate, and begged the body of Jesus. Then Pilate commanded the body to be delivered. [59]And when Joseph had taken the body, he wrapped it in a clean linen cloth, [60]And laid it in his own new tomb, which he had hewn out in the rock: and he rolled a great stone to the door of the sepulchre, and departed. (Mathew 27:57–60)

And ye shall know the truth, and the truth shall make you free. (John 8:32)

[25]But this cometh to pass, that the word might be fulfilled that is written in their law, They hated me without a cause. [26]But when the Comforter is come, whom I will send unto you from the Father, even the Spirit of truth, which proceedeth from the Father, he shall testify of me: [27]And ye also shall bear witness, because ye have been with me from the beginning. (John 15:25–27)

[38]And after this Joseph of Arimathaea, being a disciple of Jesus, but secretly for fear of the Jews, besought Pilate that he might take away the body of Jesus: and Pilate gave him leave. He came therefore, and took the body of Jesus. [39]And there came also Nicodemus, which at the first came to Jesus by night, and brought

a mixture of myrrh and aloes, about an hundred pound weight. [40]Then took they the body of Jesus, and wound it in linen clothes with the spices, as the manner of the Jews is to bury. [41]Now in the place where he was crucified there was a garden; and in the garden a new sepulchre, wherein was never man yet laid. [42]There laid they Jesus therefore because of the Jews' preparation day; for the sepulchre was nigh at hand. (John 19:38–42)

Neither yield ye your members as instruments of unrighteousness unto sin: but yield yourselves unto God, as those that are alive from the dead, and your members as instruments of righteousness unto God. (Romans 6:13)

And not only they, but ourselves also, which have the firstfruits of the Spirit, even we ourselves groan within ourselves, waiting for the adoption, to wit, the redemption of our body. (Romans 8:23)

I beseech you therefore, brethren, by the mercies of God, that ye present your bodies a living sacrifice, holy, acceptable unto God, which is your reasonable service. (Romans 12:1)

For whether we live, we live unto the Lord; and whether we die, we die unto the Lord: whether we live therefore, or die, we are the Lord's. (Romans 14:8)

For whatsoever things were written aforetime were written for our learning, that we through patience and comfort of the scriptures might have hope. (Romans 15:4)

Know ye not that your bodies are the members of Christ? shall I then take the members of Christ, and make them the members of an harlot? God forbid. (1 Corinthians 6:15)

[19]What? know ye not that your body is the temple of the Holy Ghost which is in you, which ye have of God, and ye are not your own? [20]For ye are bought with a price: therefore glorify God in your body, and in your spirit, which are God's. (1 Corinthians 6:19–20)

But God giveth it a body as it hath pleased him, and to every seed his own body. (1 Corinthians 15:38)

⁵¹Behold, I tell you a mystery: We all shall not sleep, but we shall all be changed, ⁵²in a moment, in the twinkling of an eye, at the last trump: for the trumpet shall sound, and the dead shall be raised incorruptible, and we shall be changed. (1 Corinthians 15:51-52)

And the very God of peace sanctify you wholly; and I pray God your whole spirit and soul and body be preserved blameless unto the coming of our Lord Jesus Christ. (1 Thessalonians 5:23)

⁶But now hath he obtained a more excellent ministry, by how much also he is the mediator of a better covenant, which was established upon better promises. ⁷For if that first covenant had been faultless, then should no place have been sought for the second. ⁸For finding fault with them, he saith, Behold, the days come, saith the Lord, when I will make a new covenant with the house of Israel and with the house of Judah: ⁹Not according to the covenant that I made with their fathers in the day when I took them by the hand to lead them out of the land of Egypt; because they continued not in my covenant, and I regarded them not, saith the Lord. ¹⁰For this is the covenant that I will make with the house of Israel after those days, saith the Lord; I will put my laws into their mind, and write them in their hearts: and I will be to them a God, and they shall be to me a people: ¹¹And they shall not teach every man his neighbour, and every man his brother, saying, Know the Lord: for all shall know me, from the least to the greatest. ¹²For I will be merciful to their unrighteousness, and their sins and their iniquities will I remember no more. ¹³In that he saith, A new covenant, he hath made the first old. Now that which decayeth and waxeth old is ready to vanish away. (Hebrews 8:6–13)

By the which will we are sanctified through the offering of the body of Jesus Christ once for all. (Hebrews 10:10)

If any of you lack wisdom, let him ask of God, that giveth to all men liberally, and upbraideth not; and it shall be given him. (James 1:5)

References

Cremation Is It Christian?"; Fraser, James W.; Dubuque, IA 52004-1028; Published by ECS Ministries (2005)

The Holy Bible, Cornerstone Bible Publishers; Nashville, Tennessee 37234-0164; King James Version (1998)

Webster's *Ninth New Collegiate Dictionary"* Massachusetts; Merriam-Webster, Inc. (1988)

Thought

Lord, may I discover my loneliness so that I can then collaborate with You in the salvation of the world.

Printed in the United States
by Baker & Taylor Publisher Services